Christopher Columbus

Wendy Conklin, M.A.

Table of Contents

The Man Who Changed the World

Imagine a map of the world without North and South America. Hundreds of years ago, this was the way maps looked.

Some people thought they could go from Europe to China by traveling west. When one explorer tried this, he discovered a new land. What he found changed the world forever. This explorer was Christopher Columbus.

▼ **Ancient map of the world**

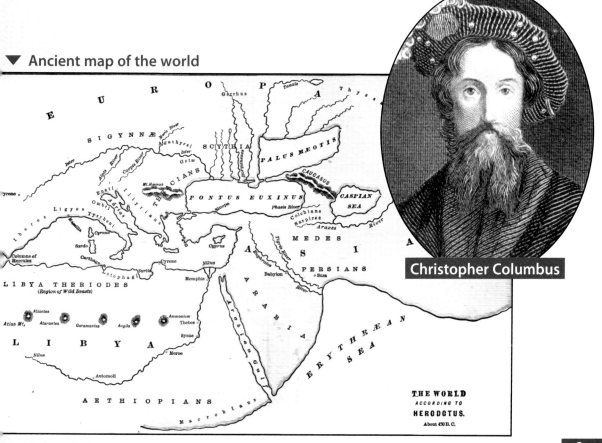

Christopher Columbus

THE WORLD
ACCORDING TO
HERODOTUS.
About 450 B.C.

In the Time of Columbus

Christopher Columbus lived in an exciting time. People were trying new things all over the world. There were great artists in Italy. Books were being printed for the first time. Learning about the world was important.

New, fast boats with large sails and big **cargo** areas were being built. Prince Henry the **Navigator** of Portugal started a school for sailors. There was no better time for an explorer.

▲ **Prince Henry discusses navigation with an explorer**

▲ Ships used for exploration

Prince Henry's School

Students in Prince Henry's school learned to use astrolabes (AS-truh-labes). An astrolabe used the stars and sun to help explorers find out where they were going.

▼ Astrolabe

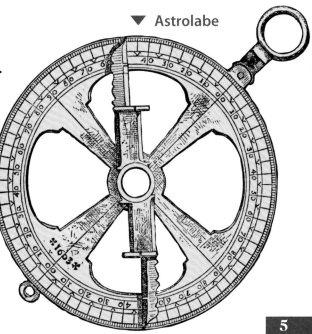

Prince Henry

Christopher Columbus

His Dreams

Christopher Columbus was born in 1451 in Genoa, Italy. Since Genoa is on the coast, it is a **port** town. Living by the water made Columbus dream of sailing one day.

A man named Marco Polo lived more than 100 years before Columbus. Polo traveled to China with his father and uncle. He wrote a very popular book about his travels.

Columbus owned a copy of Polo's book. This book made people want to explore the world.

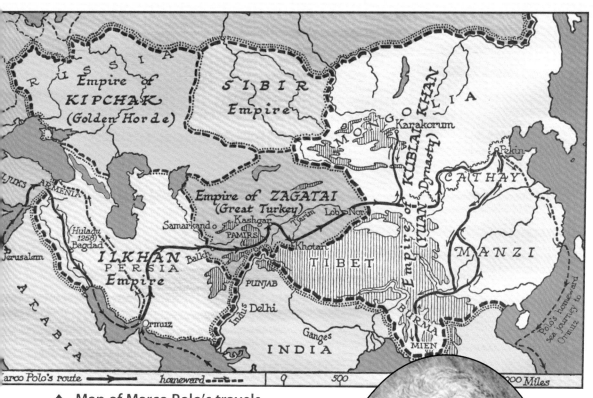

▲ Map of Marco Polo's travels

▼ Kublai Khan, a ruler of China

Marco Polo

Marco Polo's Adventures

Polo claimed that he was friends with the Chinese ruler, Kublai Khan. Khan even let Polo rule over a city!

The Size of Earth

The size of Earth was a mystery when Columbus was alive. Since no one had sailed around the world yet, no one knew how big the Earth was.

A **geographer** named Claudius Ptolemy (TOL-uh-mee) said Earth was small. Although Ptolemy was wrong, many sailors used his map of the world.

Columbus thought that European (yur-uh-PEE-uhn) ships could reach Asia by sailing west. This would take him over the Atlantic Ocean. Others thought that Earth was too large. Many feared a ship's **crew** would starve before reaching land.

▼ Map by Ptolemy

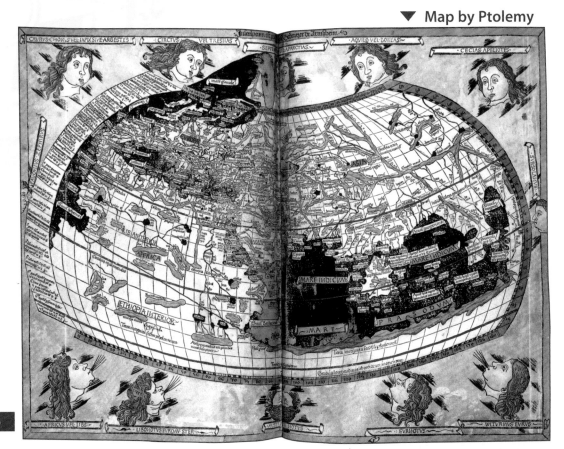

▲ Columbus discussing his theory about sailing west

Eratosthenes

A **mathematician** who lived 1,700 years before Christopher Columbus guessed the size of Earth. He was very close to the real size. Unfortunately, his ideas were forgotten for a long time.

▼ World map created by Eratosthenes

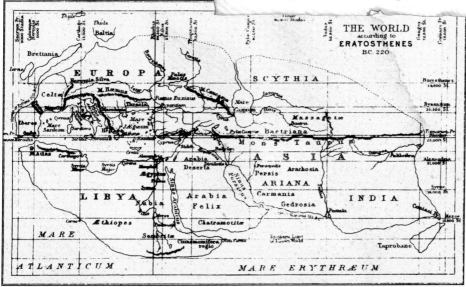

▲ Columbus honoring the king and queen

Getting Funding

A sailor needed money to make his dreams come true. Christopher Columbus tried to get money from King John of Portugal. Columbus' plan did not interest the king.

Columbus then asked King Ferdinand and Queen Isabella of Spain for help. He told them that this trip could make Spain rich. He said he would help **convert** people to Christianity.

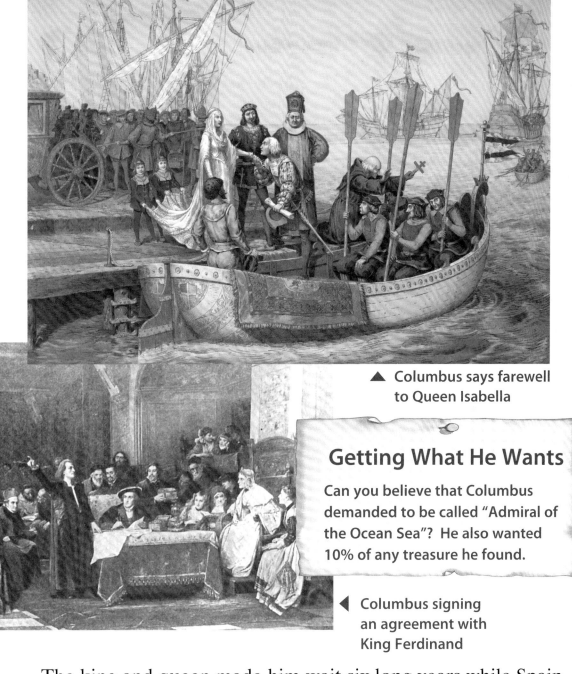

▲ Columbus says farewell to Queen Isabella

Getting What He Wants

Can you believe that Columbus demanded to be called "Admiral of the Ocean Sea"? He also wanted 10% of any treasure he found.

◀ Columbus signing an agreement with King Ferdinand

The king and queen made him wait six long years while Spain fought a war. When the war was over, they gave him three ships, supplies, and a crew.

▲ Columbus and his crew leaving Spain

Gathering a Crew

Columbus had a hard time finding men willing to sail with him. Sailors called the Atlantic Ocean the "Sea of Darkness." Other people thought giant monsters lived in the oceans.

Sailors were afraid of large **whirlpools** that could swallow their whole ship. Some men believed they would starve to death before reaching land.

Doctors, carpenters, and servants sailed as part of a crew. Columbus also took along an **interpreter** (in-TER-pruh-tuhr). This interpreter spoke many languages. Columbus hoped the interpreter would understand the people of Asia.

▼ The *Niña*, *Pinta*, and *Santa María* at sea

The Ships

The king and queen gave Columbus three ships. The fastest was the Pinta, the smallest was the Niña, and the longest was the Santa María. Columbus left Spain on August 2, 1492.

On the Sea

To make sure the crew would survive the trip, the ships had a lot of food. The ocean water was salty, so they had to take fresh water. They also brought firewood, extra sails, and **compasses**. The list of supplies was very long.

▲ The first sighting of land in the New World

◀ Compass

Seeing Land

Columbus promised that the first man to see land would get a reward. Every day, men called out that they saw land. Usually, their eyes were playing tricks on them.

▲ Columbus claiming land for Spain

Sailors had to sleep on the floors of the ship. When the trip seemed too long to handle anymore, the men **rebelled** (ri-BELD) against Captain Columbus. He begged them to give him three more days. Luckily for Columbus, the crew soon spotted land and went ashore.

Landing in the New World

The crew on the *Niña* was the first to spot land. Columbus believed he had reached Asia, but he was wrong. His ships had found an island in the Bahamas.

Since Columbus thought he was in the Indies, he called the natives, "Indians." Columbus gave the natives beaded necklaces and small bells. In return, the natives gave the crew unusual fruits and bread.

▼ **Map of the Bahamas**

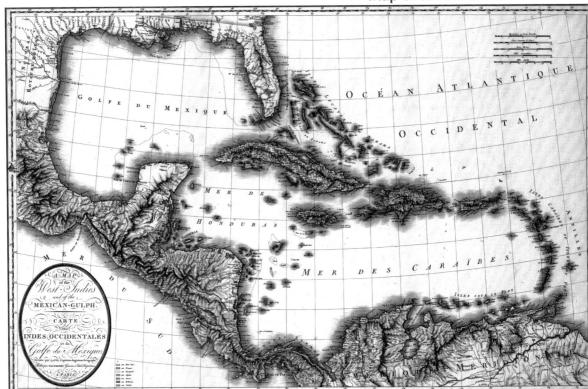

The Bahamas

The three ships landed in the Bahamas in the Caribbean (kuh-RIB-ee-uhn) Sea. Columbus' men explored two different islands.

Columbus noticed that the natives wore gold nose rings. He used hand signals to find out where they found the gold. Remember, he got to keep 10% of whatever treasure he could find.

▲ Columbus interacting with island natives

Explorers and the Natives

It did not take long for the crew to mistreat the natives. They kidnapped the women and stole gold. When the natives refused to convert to Christianity, the crew sold them as slaves. If the natives could not find gold, they were punished or killed.

Eclipse

Columbus told the natives that if they did not give him food, he would block the moon. He had read sky charts and knew that an eclipse (eh-KLIPS) was going to happen. When it did, the natives were very scared.

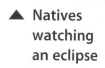

▲ Natives watching an eclipse

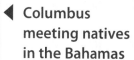

◀ Columbus meeting natives in the Bahamas

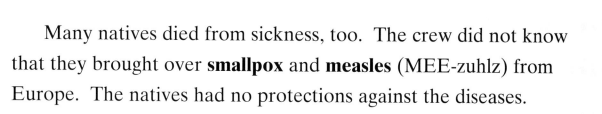

Many natives died from sickness, too. The crew did not know that they brought over **smallpox** and **measles** (MEE-zuhlz) from Europe. The natives had no protections against the diseases.

Columbus' Other Voyages

Columbus made four journeys to the New World. The king and queen wanted to create a **settlement** (SET-uhl-muhnt) there. On his second trip, Columbus took 17 ships and 1,500 men. Six priests also went to convert the natives.

▲ Columbus sharing what he discovered on his voyage with the king and queen of Spain

▲ Columbus in a Spanish prison

After his third journey, Columbus was arrested in Spain. He had treated the natives too harshly.

The queen forgave him and sent him out a fourth time. Worms ate his ship and it had too many holes to sail. He had to land on an island. Other ships later rescued him.

New Signature

After his first trip to the New World, Columbus signed his name in a new way. These Latin words meant "Christ-bearer."

How Columbus Made History

Columbus did not find a new route to Asia, but he did make history. New maps were drawn that included the Americas.

After him, other men sailed there looking for gold and land. They took horses, bees, peaches, and sugar from Europe to this new land. For the first time Europeans tasted chocolate and corn sent over from the New World.

Map of the South American coast ▶

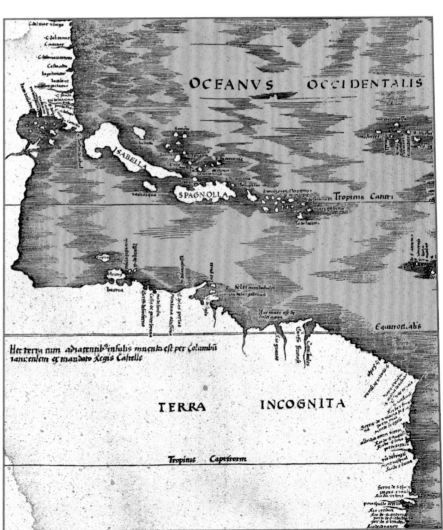

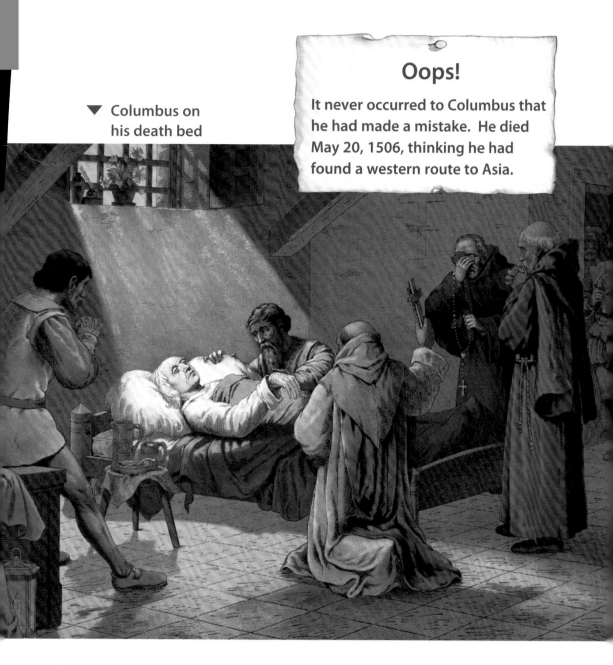

▼ Columbus on his death bed

Oops!

It never occurred to Columbus that he had made a mistake. He died May 20, 1506, thinking he had found a western route to Asia.

Life for the natives was never the same, either. Settlers soon followed the explorers. When the settlers built their homes, the natives lost their land. Columbus' trips caused many changes for people all over the world.

Glossary

astrolabes—instruments that measure navigation using the sun and stars

cargo—goods that are carried on a ship

compasses—instruments that show geographic directions

convert—to make someone change beliefs

crew—the people who work on a ship

eclipse—when the sun or moon is blocked from view

geographer—a person who studies Earth and it features

interpreter—someone who can speak more than one language

Khan, Kublai—emperor of China from 1215–1294, founder of the Yüan dynasty

Latin—language from ancient Rome

mathematician—someone who studies mathematics

measles—a sickness that produces red spots on the skin

navigator—a sea explorer

port—town on the water where ships load and unload cargo

rebelled—fought against a leader

settlement—people from another country living in a new place

smallpox—a deadly sickness

whirlpools—dangerous water flowing in fast circles